Through the Eyes of

CHILDREN

RUSSIA

Connie Bickman

Published by Abdo & Daughters, 4940 Viking Drive, Suite 622, Edina, Minnesota 55435.

Library bound edition distributed by Rockbottom Books, Pentagon Tower, P.O. Box 36036, Minneapolis, Minnesota 55435.

Printed in the United States.

Cover Photo credit: Connie Bickman
Interior Photo credits: Connie Bickman
Map created by John Hamilton

Edited By Julie Berg

LIBRARY OF CONGRESS CATALOGING-IN-PUBLICATION DATA

Bickman, Connie.
    Russia / Connie Bickman.
        p.   cm. -- (Through the Eyes of Children)
    Includes bioliographical references and index.
    ISBN 1-56239-329-4
    1. Russia (Federation)--Description and travel--Juvenile literature. [1. Russia (Federation)--Social life and customs.]
    I. Title.II. Series.
    DK510.29.8531994
    947--dc20   94-19299
                                            CIP
                                            AC

Contents

Introduction to Russia

Russia is the largest country in the world.
It is more than twice the size of the United States.
On the map, it is shaped like a giant steer.
Its tail-like peninsula dips into the Bering Sea.
Its eye is the city of Moscow.
The country is so big that there is an eleven hour
time difference between eastern and western Russia.
Russia also has many different kinds of land within
its borders.

RUSSIA

St. Petersburg
Moscow
Nizhniy Novgorod
Volga River
Kazan
Samara
Ural Mountains
Ob River
Rostov-na-Donu
Volgograd
Yekaterinburg
Chelyabinsk
SIBERIA
Magadan
Lena
Novosibirsk
Krasnoyarsk
Irkutsk
Vladivostok

1,500 miles

Population
148.9 Million

Area (square miles)
6,592,819

City Population
● Over 8 million
● Over 4 million
● Over 1 million
○ Under 1 million
Capital: Moscow

It could be 100 degrees with camel caravans traveling across the desert, and a freezing -70 degrees in northern Siberia in the Arctic Circle—all at the same time!

There are many rivers and canals that are used for shipping. They link the country to five separate seas.

A famous river there is the Volga River.

You will find many different kinds of people as you cross the land.

They have different customs and lifestyles.

In the northern forests, people fish, trap furs, and farm.

Nomads pitch their tents across the southern steppe or prairie lands.

They are great horsemen who live off the land.

There are country people and city people.

And there are people a lot like you and your family!

Meet the Children

These children have curious smiles on their faces.
They are usually very shy.
Most of the Russian people have to work very hard.
So do the children.
They don't have a lot of time for play and laughter.
Some children are luckier than others.
They have a chance to take dance and music lessons.
Russia is proud of its art culture.

What's Good to Eat?

This lady is working in a store in a small country village.
There is not much food on the shelves.
She has boxed food, jars of vegetables, and fresh bread.

The lady does not have a cash register or a calculator.
Instead she uses an abacus for counting.
It is made of wood beads on a wire frame.
When you shop in the store, you do not get bags for your groceries.
You must bring your own paper bag.

Food—especially meat—is often hard to find in Russia.
The people eat a lot of soup.
It is called borsch.
It is made with cabbage and beets.
It is served hot or cold.
They also eat cabbage salad, breads, meat pies (pirogi), and potatoes.
Food served at an expensive Russian buffet is much different.
It could include smoked fish, stuffed hams, roast chicken, salads, and pies.

Many of the people in Moscow were glad to get a McDonalds restaurant!
They know they will find meat there.
These people are lined up around a big city block.
They are waiting to get in to eat.

What Do They Wear?

Do you think this boy's hat is warm?
It is made of rabbit skin.
It is very soft and warm.
The flaps keep his ears and neck warm.
The people wear wool clothing to keep warm.
It gets very cold in the winter.
There are many sudden rain showers in the summer.
You will see a lot of umbrellas during that time.

Where Do They Live?

There are not many houses in the city.
Most of the people live in big apartment
buildings like this one.
The rooms are small because there are so many
apartments in each building.
Sometimes it gets very crowded.

This big green house is in a country village.
It has fancy wood carvings around the doors and windows.
Many of the houses are painted in bright colors.
It makes the village look cheery during the long, cold winter.

The wooden houses in this village are surrounded by fences.
The family chops wood to heat the house.
In the summertime, the yard is filled with beautiful flowers.

Getting Around

Riding a bike in Russia is an inexpensive way to get around.
Sometimes children travel many miles on their bikes.
These boys are coming home from school.

Cars, buses, trains, and trolleys are ways to travel in Russia.
The "underground" is the best way to travel in the big cities.
It is a train that travels through tunnels under the streets.
Horses and wagons are another way to travel.
This man has milk cans on his wagon.
He is selling milk in the village market nearby.

School is Fun!

Do you like to make things?
These children do.
They are painting little carved animals.
These pieces of art will be sold at an art fair.
Children go to school six days a week in Russia.

There is a long wall of ceramic tiles in Moscow.
It is on Arbot Street.
Children painted messages of peace on these tiles.
They came from children all over Russia.
Do you see the one that says, "To my American Friends"?

How Do They Work?

Most of the children in Russia work very hard.
They help support their families.
Some work on small farms.
Some sell things on the city streets.
This boy is an entertainer.
He is playing the accordion.
He has a little dish in which people put money.

Their Land

When you travel through parts of Russia,
you will see buildings that look like castles.
Some people call these roofs onion domes.
They are churches and cathedrals.
These buildings are called Rostov Kremlin.
They have gold paint on their domes that shine in
the sunlight.
This is one of the oldest towns of northern Russia.
Many buildings also have museums with famous
artwork.
Inside are statues and gold carvings and beautiful
paintings.

This church is in a city called Zagorsk. It is in an area called the Golden Ring. The Golden Ring is made up of a group of ancient cities. You will learn a lot about Russia's history when you visit these cities.

Animals Are Friends

Dogs are very popular animals in Russia.
Russia also has cats and hamsters, guniea pigs
and cows.
There are also wild animals such as deer and
bear in Russia.

Life in the City

Moscow is a big city.
Its name is sometimes known as the
"Mother of the People."
This famous church is called St. Basil's
Cathedral.
Its carved wooden domes are very old.
No two spiraled domes are alike.
It is on Red Square in Moscow.
Red Square means "beautiful square" in
old Russian.
It once was a marketplace.
The Kremlin is also near Red Square.
The word Kremlin means fortress.
The government rules the country from
the Kremlin.

This girl is bundled up to go shopping with her family.
There is a big store called GUM department store.
It is owned by the government.
Only things made in Russia are sold there.
Usually there are long lines of people waiting to shop in the store.
And usually there is not very much to buy.
Maybe she will go to the toy store instead!

These men own a store in the city.
They are painting a new sign.
Inside the store, they sell wooden toys for children.
The toys are made in a village near Zagorsk.

Family Living

This boy and his dad are taking a walk.
They are on a street in Moscow.
Do you see the writing on the building?
It is all written in Russian.
Children like to write their names on the wall.
Sometimes artists draw pictures on the wall.

Getting a ride on dad's shoulders is fun.
It means
this girl
can get a
better view
of the
park.
Her
matching
hat and
coat looks
very
warm.
What do
you think
she has in
her purse?

This mother and grandmother are out for a walk.
They are pushing a buggy called a pram.
The baby is snuggled inside to keep warm.
The grandmother has a tin jar in her hand.
She is going to the store to get milk.

What are Traditions?

These soldiers are marching.
They are kicking their legs very high.
They are marching to Lenin's tomb.
Two soldiers must stand guard by the tomb at all times.
It is a tradition.
The tomb is where Lenin is buried.
He was a famous Russian leader.

When people get married in Russia,
there are many traditions.
One is to bring flowers to the Tomb of
the Unknown Soldier.
A flame burns
there all the
time.
It is called the
eternal flame.

Dancing and singing are favorite traditions in Russia.
These girls are wearing colorful costumes.
They are singing old Russian folk songs.
The songs are about the land and the people.
The songs also tell about hopes for the children of
Russia.

Just for Fun

Do you like to play in the snow?
These boys are having a snowball fight.
They were also building a snowman.
Ice skating and playing in the snow are favorite things to do in Russia.
That is because there is usually a lot of snow!
Another fun thing is the Moscow circus.
There are a lot of animals and daring acts to watch.
If you like to dance, you could go to the famous Bolshoi Theater.
Children learn to dance at a young age.
They must work very hard to become a ballet dancer.

Children are the same everywhere

It is fun to see how children in other countries live. Many children have similar ways of doing things. Did you see things that were the same as in your life? They may play and go to school and have families just like you. They may work, travel and dress different than you.

One thing is always the same. That is a smile. If you smile at other children, they will smile back. That is how you make new friends. It's fun to have new friends all over the world!

GLOSSARY

Abacus - Wooden beads on a wire frame used for counting.

Borsch - A soup made from cabbage and beets.

Kremlin - A fortress or city with walls all around it.

Nomads - Tribes of people that move from place to place to find pasture for their cattle.

Pirogi - Meat pies.

Tundra - Frozen, treeless land in the Arctic.

Underground - Train that travels through tunnels under the streets.

Index

About the Author/Photographer

Connie Bickman is a photojournalist whose photography has won regional and international awards.

She is retired from a ten-year newspaper career and currently owns her own portrait studio and art gallery. She is an active freelance photographer and writer whose passion it is to travel the far corners of the world in search of adventure and the opportunity to photograph native cultures.

She is a member of the National Press Association and the Minnesota Newspaper Photographers Association.